JPIC Sch
Schuette W9-AQK-613
Color camouflage : a
spot-it challenge

$25.99
ocn671704833
01/16/2012

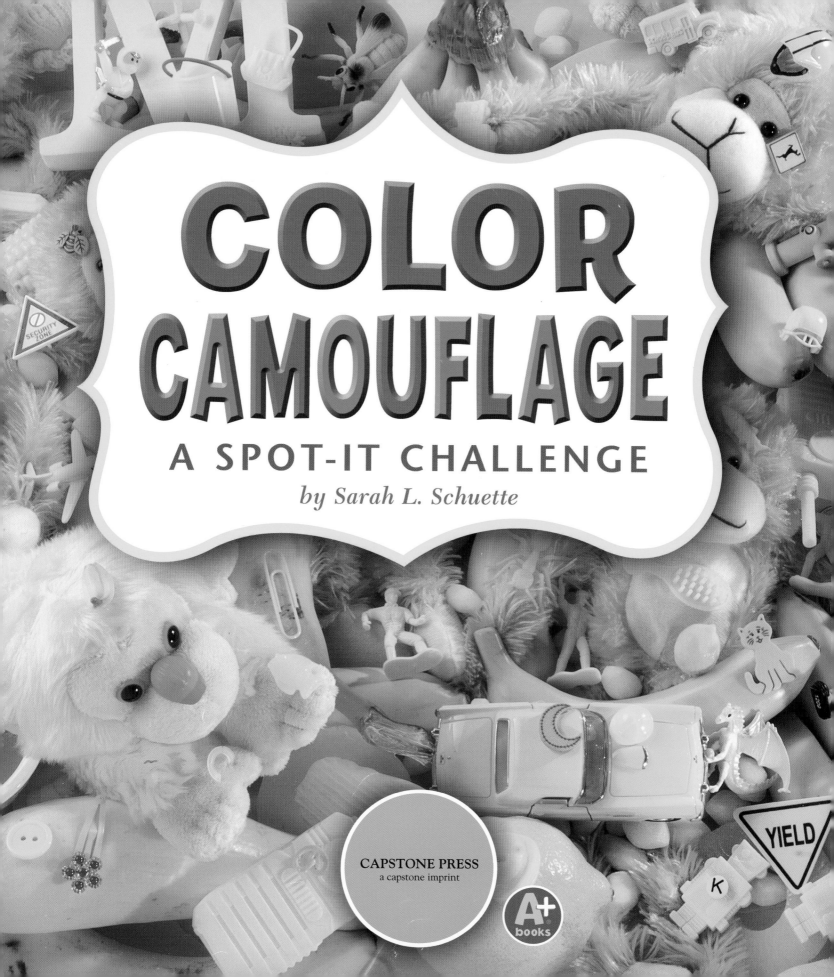

COLOR CAMOUFLAGE

A SPOT-IT CHALLENGE

by Sarah L. Schuette

CAPSTONE PRESS
a capstone imprint

A+
books

A+ Books are published by Capstone Press,
1710 Roe Crest Drive, North Mankato, Minnesota 56003.
www.capstonepub.com

Books published by Capstone Press are manufactured with paper
containing at least 10 percent post-consumer waste.

Library of Congress Cataloging-in-Publication Data
Schuette, Sarah L., 1976–
  Color camouflage : a spot-it challenge / by Sarah L. Schuette.
    p. cm.—(A+ books. Spot it)
  Includes bibliographical references.
  Summary: "Simple text invites the reader to find items hidden in color-themed photographs"—
Provided by publisher.
  ISBN 978-1-4296-5262-9 (library binding)
  1. Puzzles—Juvenile literature. 2. Picture puzzles—Juvenile literature. I. Title. II. Series: Spot it.
  GV1493.S3164 2011
  793.73—dc22   2010045329

Credits

Jenny Marks and Gillia Olson, editors; Ted Williams, designer; Laura Manthe,
    production specialist; Sarah Schuette, photo stylist; Marcy Morin, photo scheduler

Photo Credits

all photos by Capstone Studio/Karon Dubke

The author dedicates this book in memory of her father, Willmar "Butch" Schuette.

Note to Parents, Teachers, and Librarians
Spot It is an interactive series that supports literacy development and reading enjoyment.
Readers utilize visual discrimination skills to find objects among fun-to-peruse photographs
with busy backgrounds. Readers also build vocabulary through thematic groupings, develop
visual memory ability through repeated readings, and improve strategic and associative
thinking skills by experimenting with different visual search methods.

Printed in the United States of America in North Mankato, Minnesota.
102011   006417R

Table of Contents

Orange

Can you spot . . .

- an umbrella?
- a hammer?
- a shirt?
- three cars?
- two seahorses?
- a moon?

4

Pink

Can you spot . . .

- a clothespin?
- a fly?
- a giraffe?
- two pigs?
- a lemon slice?
- a triangle?

Gray

Can you spot . . .

- a trumpet?
- a dragon?
- a fish?
- a fighter plane?
- a robot?
- a koala?

Green

Can you spot . . .

- a soda can?
- a watering can?
- a palm tree?
- a windsurfer?
- a dragonfly?
- two pine trees?

Red

Can you spot . . .

- an ant?
- a rooster?
- a candy cane?
- a checker?
- a purse?
- a chainsaw?

12

13

Yellow

Can you spot . . .

- a spray bottle?
- a fire hydrant?
- a pretzel?
- two crayons?
- a sun?
- two cupids?

Purple

Can you spot . . .

- a broom?
- a lipstick?
- a pumpkin?
- a pineapple?
- a candle?
- an ice skate?

Blue

Can you spot . . .

- a birdhouse?
- a frying pan?
- a knight?
- a teddy bear?
- a jellyfish?
- two unicorns?

Brown

Can you spot . . .
- a log cabin?
- a turkey?
- a mousetrap?
- a guitar?
- a penny?
- a walrus?

White

Can you spot . . .

○ a thumbtack?

○ a bathtub?

○ a half sandwich?

○ a prince?

○ a seal?

○ two geese?

Black

Can you spot . . .

- a pair of scissors?
- a lighthouse?
- a toaster?
- a laptop computer?
- a whistle?
- a pirate hat?

Rainbow

Can you spot . . .

- a shamrock?
- a hummingbird?
- a pickle slice?
- a fortune cookie?
- a globe?
- a letter "O"?

Spot Even More!

Orange

Try to find a helicopter, an astronaut, a spider, three traffic cones, two bowling pins, and two cats.

Pink

Take another look to find two wrenches, a hot dog, three gifts, a bone, a cookie cutter, and the letter "J."

Gray

See if you can spot a jingle bell, a cowboy, two paper clips, a tombstone, and the Eiffel Tower.

Green

This time find a sleigh, a number "2," two hearts, a cactus, two dollar signs, and two aliens.

Red

Check for some French fries, two train engines, a watch, a cake, an anchor, and a skateboard.

Yellow

Now look for a trophy, a tennis ball, a dump truck, two walkie-talkies, and the number "4."

Purple

Try to spot a set of golf clubs, a turtle, a stack of school books, and a witch's hat.

Blue

See if you can find two mittens, a blue ribbon, a snail, and a baseball cap.

Brown

Try to find a musical note, a lantern, a cowboy boot, two baseball bats, and a treasure chest.

White

See if you can spot a roll of toilet paper, an igloo, a crutch, a milk jug, and three golf balls.

Black

Now spot a screw, an ax, a nail, a thimble, and a stingray.

Rainbow

It's time to find a paintbrush, a pair of sunglasses, a gumball machine, a rabbit, and a rose.

Extreme Spot-It Challenge

Just can't get enough Spot-It action?
Here's an extra challenge. Try to spot:

- a dress
- a flamingo
- a shell
- a ninja
- a pair of ballet slippers
- a tomato
- a party hat
- a goldfish
- a chick
- a slice of watermelon
- two airplanes
- two shovels
- a bobber
- a scuba mask
- a wizard
- a pair of chopsticks
- two gift bows

Read More

Chedru, Delphine. *Spot It Again!: Find More Hidden Creatures.* New York: Abrams Books for Young Readers, 2011.

Marks, Jennifer L. *Fun and Games: A Spot-it Challenge.* Spot It! Mankato, Minn.: Capstone, 2009.

Schuette, Sarah L. *Animal Fun: A Spot-it Challenge.* Spot It! Mankato, Minn.: Capstone, 2011.

Internet Sites

FactHound offers a safe, fun way to find Internet sites related to this book. All of the sites on FactHound have been researched by our staff.

Here's all you do:

Visit *www.facthound.com*

Type in this code: **9781429652629**

Check out projects, games and lots more at
www.capstonekids.com